The Silver Linings Course Correction Guide: Your Nurturing Journey Begins Now is the companion workbook to *Silver Linings: The Essential Guide to Building Courage, Self-Respect and Wellness*, by Leaha Mattinson.

To order copies of *Silver Linings* or *The Silver Linings Course Correction Guide*, please visit http://reallifetraining.com.

Sick of Stress and Suffering? Join the *Leaha Life* Community.

We live in a world of stress, uncertainty, fear, and self-disdain, and it is taking a serious toll on our physical, mental, and emotional health. Too many people struggle through each day feeling alone, burned out, damaged, battered, and bruised. This is no way to live.

If you're ready for a course correction, visit http://reallifetraining.com to become part of the *Leaha Life* online community today. Together, we will discover and share powerful ideas and techniques for creating lives of love and peace.

We are a diverse group of people dedicated to empowerment, joy, and total wellness. Full of inspiring articles, webinars, and other healing resources, our online community will help you find the answers you've been looking for (and more!). Stop the suffering cycle today and join us on a nurturing journey to create the life you want.

The Silver Linings
Course Correction Guide

Your Nurturing Journey Starts Now

Leaha Mattinson

BALBOA.
PRESS

A DIVISION OF HAY HOUSE

Balboa Press books may be ordered through booksellers or by contacting:

Balboa Press
A Division of Hay House
1663 Liberty Drive
Bloomington, IN 47403
www.balboapress.com
1 (877) 407-4847

Because of the dynamic nature of the Internet, any web addresses or links contained in this book may have changed since publication and may no longer be valid. The views expressed in this work are solely those of the author and do not necessarily reflect the views of the publisher, and the publisher hereby disclaims any responsibility for them.

The author of this book does not dispense medical advice or prescribe the use of any technique as a form of treatment for physical, emotional, or medical problems without the advice of a physician, either directly or indirectly. The intent of the author is only to offer information of a general nature to help you in your quest for emotional and spiritual well-being. In the event you use any of the information in this book for yourself, which is your constitutional right, the author and the publisher assume no responsibility for your actions.

Any people depicted in stock imagery provided by Thinkstock are models, and such images are being used for illustrative purposes only. Certain stock imagery © Thinkstock.

Print information available on the last page.

ISBN: 978-1-5043-7101-8 (sc)
ISBN: 978-1-5043-7150-6 (e)

Library of Congress Control Number: 2016920585

Balboa Press rev. date: 12/12/2016

Introduction

A friend of mine who is a pilot once shared with me a lesson he learned in his flight training classes. He explained that any pilot embarking on a journey from Point A to Point B always begins their trip by charting a course—a straight line from their current location to where they want to land. However, my pilot pal revealed that more often than not, the plane usually veers *off course* rather than remaining on track. In fact, the pilot's primary job is to "right" the voyage by constantly steering the plane back to its charted path.

I believe this plane analogy is a metaphor for the trek we all are on in life. At some point each of us will face unexpected plot twists, disappointments, stresses, and struggles that could derail our journey and leave us hopelessly lost. When these perfect storms appear, it may seem impossible to find the horizon, reorient ourselves, and get back on route.

Here is the truth: You can and must correct your own course. Storms are a guaranteed part of life. But what you choose to do, say, think, and feel in the thunder and lightning will determine the quality of your journey and the journey of those around you. *The Silver Linings Course Correction Guide* is a compass to help you assess where you are right now and determine where you would like to be. It provides the tools to get back on course and live a brave, integrity-driven, full-hearted life.

The following exercises are inspired by topics discussed in *Silver Linings: The Essential Guide to Building Courage, Self-Respect and Wellness.* Feel free to complete them as you read *Silver Linings* or explore them separately any time you need a healthy dose of direction and love.

Think about the role judgment plays in determining your life experiences. Do you perpetually live on a hair trigger, ready to negatively judge every event in your day? How would someone else describe your primary state of mind? Consider how constant judgment influences your state of mind and your health. In the space provided, write down your five biggest judgment "triggers" and how they affect your overall wellness. (These judgments could be against yourself or others.) Then for one week, try to suspend all judgment and see what you learn about its effect on your life. Journal daily about how you did with this experiment to keep yourself on course.

So much suffering comes from fear-driven choices. It is very difficult to choose love over fear (especially when facing crises like illness, heartbreak, addiction, or death) but the rewards of doing so are immense. For one day, keep track of the fear-driven choices you make. You may realize that you've been playing it safe, avoiding uncomfortable situations, and suffering in silence, all out of...you guessed it, fear. In the space below, complete the sentence "If I stopped making fear-based decisions, here's how my life would change..."

Self-esteem is something everyone wants but many are unclear on how to "get" it. Here is the way: Pick a small, achievable task for yourself—say, deciding to make your bed each day—and then, no matter what, do the "thing" you've chosen each day without fail. Your bedrock of self-esteem continues growing as you constantly fulfill your agreements with yourself. What will be your first small, achievable goal?

_____

_____

_____

_____

_____

_____

_____

_____

_____

_____

_____

_____

Times of adversity are shadow initiations that can either teach us what we're made of or ensnare us in an undertow of pain. Spend a few moments thinking about the worst thing that has ever happened to you (don't wallow in the memory—just observe it without attaching any feeling to it). Now see if you can recognize how this event influenced your soul, for better or worse. Are you stronger than you were before? What did you learn? How did it shape who you are today? Write your discoveries below.

At one point or another, we all get "stuck" in life—it's a normal occurrence, but too often, we stay stuck instead of moving on through the present challenge. Think about a life situation or circumstance in which you are "stuck" right now. Symptoms of being stuck might include resentment, rigid thoughts, fears, and other roadblocks that prevent you from making healthy choices for your life. Here's a thought sample of someone who is stuck: *Right now I am so angry at (my sibling/ my friend/my workplace) that I can barely function. I can't get past this. I am consumed in rage/sorrow/grief/stress.* In the space below, write down a topic or situation that has you "stuck" and list the factors you must work through in order to get "un-stuck." What are your limiting thoughts? Who must you forgive in order to move on? What do you need to release? How and when are you going to do what needs to be done? What's the benefit to you in staying stuck?

Your morning mindset drastically influences your whole day. An energizing morning ritual can help you get in a positive head space by preparing your mind and body for a day of joy and positivity. On the lines below, list a few steps you can take to create a personalized ten-minute morning protocol to jumpstart your day. Here are a few suggestions to get you started: speak uplifting affirmations to yourself and those in your life, breathe in and out slowly while focusing on gratitude, pray, create loving intentions, perform sun salutations, quietly sip a cup of herbal tea, read a daily devotion, crank the tunes and do a happy/silly/sexy dance, etc. What will your morning ritual look like?

Has letting yourself down left you *feeling down*? We often hold ourselves to a higher standard than other people and use these standards as guidelines for measuring our self-worth. We also often break our word to ourselves, which causes a different kind of wound—a soul wound—because our souls cannot live in untruth. That's why it is so difficult to bounce back when you give up too early, fail, or otherwise fall short in some way. It's also why we feel pressured during these moments, because we are pursued by the truth. Describe a time that you let yourself down and how it has damaged your self-worth. What do you need to do to release the self-blame? Maybe you owe someone an apology, or need to stand up and keep trying, or maybe you need to walk away from an old goal that no longer fits in your life. No matter what course of action is required, know that confronting your feelings of disappointment and getting truthful with yourself about the reality of what you are doing (and moving it in closer alignment with your true vision for yourself) will instantly put you on the road to peace and healing.

Our parents give us life, along with a multitude of unconventional "gifts." These "gifts" aren't always packaged the way we expect or want them to be, but they are nonetheless ours to live with and learn from. They come in the form of parental mistakes, hard lessons to learn, unwelcomed genetic inheritances, and a bevy of challenges passed down through both nurture and nature. On the lines provided, list some of the unconventional gifts you received from your parents. This exercise is NOT about blame or dwelling in negativity. Instead it is a way to feel gratitude for the person you became as a result of their gifts. Be brave enough to acknowledge the honest positive outcomes of these gifts. I guarantee you that if you look, you can find the blessing in any adversity.

An example of one of these "gifts" might be: *The "gift" of neglect. My parents both worked long hours, and I had to spend many parts of my childhood by myself. This helped me become self-reliant. Today, I know that if I am bored, sad, angry, or distraught, I have the resources to pull myself out of a bad place, to nurture myself in healthy ways, and feel better immediately. Their long working hours also taught me a work ethic AND showed me how much they loved me.*

Too many people fail to live up to their potential. As a result, they have dreams and goals that go unexplored and unachieved. When we settle for less than we truly desire, we sell ourselves short and miss out on fulfillment. We also miss out on fulfilling our purpose. What if you were meant to do something really amazing that would have influenced the world for goodness and you decided to stay in your room instead? What is the impact on your family when you quit growing? What kind of role model are you to your children? Realize that you can truly manifest anything you want out of life by developing a combination of faith and a growth mindset, which helps you discover your goals and work methodically to achieve them, and to keep working to achieve them even when there is adversity! What would you do differently if you started living up to your potential TODAY? What would it change in your life? In your family's life? Below, write about what living up to your potential means for you, and then list your first step toward achieving a dream or goal that you have right now.

_____

_____

_____

_____

_____

_____

_____

_____

A solid work ethic will take you far in life, both career-wise and in relation to your life goals and personal development. Remember, though, that your "work" is so much more than the job you do for money. Your work is your life's purpose—what you are here to do. Many people hide from their "work" through laziness, disconnection, or flat-out avoidance. If you currently don't possess a stellar work ethic, don't worry! You can develop a healthy attitude about work and then watch your dreams (and often your purpose as well!) blossom before your eyes. In the space below, write an honest assessment of your current work habits (no fibbing allowed!). What changes would bring you in alignment with your ideal work ethic? What sacrifices can you make to allow more dedication to your "work"?

Have you ever had a negative emotional reaction that didn't make sense to you at the time? When you find yourself snapping at or being short with friends, family, or coworkers, close your mouth and delve into your emotions and figure out what is really causing your behavior. Are you secretly jealous, resentful, suppressing fear, or dealing with a combination of other emotion-driven factors? The next time you ask yourself, *Why did I just feel that?!* take a moment to assess what is really driving your feelings. Below, list some emotions that trigger the desire to participate in irrational behavior for you. What are some steps you can take to alleviate these emotions? How can you stop yourself in your tracks, before you say something or do something you can't take back?

When you are overwhelmed with too many commitments, time demands, or your own "stuff" (like an illness or a personal crisis), life suddenly seems undoable. During times like these, it is essential to scale back to basics and cut out all the unnecessary "noise" of life. For you, this could mean canceling an upcoming visit or trip, turning off the television and radio, or ordering takeout for a few days until the chaos subsides. The next time your life speeds into overdrive, what will you cut out so you can get back to basics? What do the "basics" mean to you?

Laughter is powerful medicine that can actually make you feel better after a rotten day (or week!). Luckily we can all choose to laugh anytime we wish—it's free and easy. The next time you want to just cry from stress, frustration, or fear, make a choice to try to lighten up instead. (Remember, you can always have a cry later if you *have* to!) Watch a funny sitcom you enjoy, call up a friend who always makes you laugh, or do something that you know will bring on healing laughter. In the space below, describe how a good laugh makes you feel physically and emotionally.

Hugging is also powerful medicine that makes you feel better any time. Like laughter, it's free and easy. I really take advantage of hugging my grandson (he is just two years old and is good for at least a three-minute full-on squish), my hubby, my kids when they'll let me, my parents, friends, and, yes...even clients! There was a little song my daughter sang when she was in preschool 16 years ago, titled "Four Hugs a Day." This is the song that I still sing today even during training sessions for adults: "Four hugs a day, that's the minimum. Four hugs a day, NOT the maximum. Four hugs a daaaaaay!" How long has it been since you gave or received a really good hug? In the space below, write down the names of those in your life you could hug right now. How could you routinely give four hugs a day? How would a hug make you feel physically and emotionally?

Resiliency, or "grit," is what allows you to bounce back from life's misfortunes and disappointments. And guess what? Life is full of these, so it's a great thing to accept this fact and get good at handling setbacks! You develop grit from overcoming difficulty. So the next time you feel yourself reeling from adversity, take a breath and a step back, and remind yourself that there may be an upside to the challenge at hand—even if you can't see it at the time. Use the space below to list five challenging moments in your life that helped you develop resiliency and courage. How did you feel about yourself when you overcame the challenge?

Choosing forgiveness is one of the most powerful choices we can make. First, it bestows grace on the person you are forgiving. Second, forgiveness actually begins with our ability to forgive ourselves and *then* spreads to others. It is the *healthiest* choice for you because it involves a release of negative emotions and memories. Forgiveness frees up space in your mind, spirit, and soul to let love fully in. In the space provided below, describe how you feel physically and emotionally whenever you hold a grudge, or when you don't forgive yourself. Then describe how you feel after you've forgiven. Notice the differences. Which choice makes you feel more powerful?

Generosity and servitude are genuinely good qualities to possess—as long as you also remember the counterbalance of taking care of yourself! Don't be a martyr! Stop putting everyone else's needs before your own. You won't be able to help anyone else if you're exhausted and burnt out from self-neglect. In fact, if you really cared about other people, you'd work just as hard to be well so you can give them everything you've got from a very healthy place! In the space below, write about how you will take care of yourself starting today. Let your intuition guide you as to what you need in order to restore yourself—whether it is a vacation, a half hour of alone time each day, or a class that interests you.

Living in alignment with your integrity isn't always easy, but it is always the right decision. If you are out of alignment with your values and personal code of conduct, you may notice your conscience tapping you on the shoulder and asking, *What's going on?* Creating an integrity blueprint can give you a good idea of your desired direction in life. What are your values? Can you name 10? Do you live by your values or do you struggle to live in alignment? What gets in the way? What could you change right this moment that would bring your values and behavior into alignment? How does that feel? (Some examples of values could be honesty, loyalty, reliability, courage, etc.)

_____

_____

_____

_____

_____

_____

_____

_____

_____

_____

_____

Feelings of entitlement are like anchors that drag you down and make you focus heavily on what's missing in your life and on what other people have. Think of the disappointment and negative energy you feel when your expectations don't line up with your reality. Do you really need that additional strife and drama in your life? Remember that you are entitled to smile all day long, to be kind and compassionate, but the world really does not owe you anything in return. It's a bonus when you get a smile back, but it is not a right. Instead of ruminating on things you want and don't have, focus on your blessings, and focus on giving. In the space below, write a list of things you are truly grateful for. (It may be longer than you expect it to be!) To continue this habit, I like to write in a journal for five minutes each day for 26 days, using a letter in the alphabet that day as my guide. So for the first day all the words should start with the letter "A," on the second day, the letter "B," and so on. You'll be amazed by the gems you'll discover while writing each day, so put in the time and *feel* the results! After the 26 days, do your blessings journaling however you wish; by then the habit will be ingrained.

Your choices make up your life, so be sure that every choice you make anchors you in goodness, peace, and love. Think about how much of your time you lend to shadow emotions like anger, resentment, and jealousy. How are they impacting your inner and outer world? Would you feel better all the time and find more fulfillment if you allowed yourself to make choices that move you toward light instead? Of course! Use the space below to express the new choices you must make in order to live in goodness.

Dropping bad habits will profoundly improve your life. Imagine how your life would improve if you let go of your worst bad habits today and never looked back. For example, if you're addicted to food and constantly overeating, think of how great it would be if you stopped turning to food to manage your feelings. Imagine if you stopped talking about others behind their backs. Or if you quit cursing, smoking, or jumping to conclusions. In the space below, write about the bad habits you'd like to drop now—and ask yourself if there is any reason you *can't* let them go. (Hint: You can!)

Don't get so caught up in life that you forget about what really matters most: your loved ones. Everyday distractions will get in the way if you let them, so it is up to you to make time for the people who matter most. In the space below, describe how you will dedicate time for spending with your spouse, children, dear friends, and family. Whether you take time every evening with your spouse to share *only* the good things that happened that day, put your cell phone away when you get home so you can interact with your kids fully, dedicate time each month to catch up with your best friend, or take one less vacation a year so you can visit your parents instead—you can find a way to make meaningful memories with those you love.

Guilt is a tricky emotion that colors your world until you resolve it. If you have made mistakes that continue to haunt you, know that there is a way through guilt—but it isn't always easy. First, if you need to apologize to someone, do so in person, in a letter, or via a phone call. Ask for forgiveness, and then begin the healing work of forgiving yourself. You are human and imperfect, and so is everyone around you. You deserve to release old guilt, replace it with positive self-regard, and heal your heart in the process. Both you and the rest of the world need your heart to be full of love! In the space provided, describe the guilt you're holding onto. How does it make you feel and how deeply is it affecting your life? What will you do to release it? How would it make your world and the world of the people around you better if you did?

Many of us are chronic procrastinators, but we may not fully understand how deeply damaging procrastination really is. If you're the type of person who perpetually kicks projects, bills, and obligations down the road, realize that you're doing yourself a huge disservice. Facing your responsibilities head-on builds self-esteem and helps you realize that you CAN do anything you set your mind to. Resolve to *stop* procrastinating now. Bring in a trusted advisor/mentor/coach to help keep you honest. Is it easy? Not always. Worth it? Absolutely. Below, write down 10 ways you routinely procrastinate and then focus on how you're going to stop the cycle of putting things off.

You owe it to yourself to take good care of your body. How would it feel to get out of bed every single day without an ache or pain? How would it change your life if you literally never, ever got sick? Whether you're overweight, or thin but addicted to junk food, or just an unmotivated couch potato, your health is highly important to your general well-being. How can you improve your physical wellness in a way that will make you happy? Maybe you can join a fun dance or fitness class or do a pantry purge to get rid of junk food. What if nothing in the physical wellness realm makes you happy? Do something for your fitness and health anyway. Not everything in life is fun. Remember when your mom told you that? She was right. Having discipline to do the things that aren't fun, at least to start with, is what sets apart the successful from the constantly unhappy and unhealthy. Another tip: Have more sex within the context of a loving relationship. Being intimate is good in too many ways to even mention, and it is another good way to take care of your body. Or…what if you grew a garden full of fresh organic veggies or stopped watching so much television and got some fresh air instead? List your thoughts and ideas below.

_____

_____

_____

_____

_____

_____

_____

We are gifted with life for only a short while in the grand scheme of things, so it is important to be present for the day—and the moment—at hand and try not to worry about the future and the past. If you're like most of us, you likely spend much of your time dwelling on the past or worrying about the future. How much time do you devote to the "now"? For one day, concentrate on remaining in the present. Each time you catch yourself slipping into a memory or leaping to the future, gently guide yourself back. In the space below, reflect on your experience being in the now. How is it different?

Sweetheart,

Now that you have toiled through this guide and stretched yourself with these exercises, I know that you're ready to navigate where you're headed from here. First, know this in your soul: You are amazing…simply because you exist.

So, starting from that place, you get to decide…what do you really want for your life? Maybe you've never realized that within you lies the power to create the world you desire for yourself, over and over again. Even if right now you're so far off course that you can't imagine ever finding your way back, know that you are not alone and that you have everything you need inside of you to arrive safely at a destination of love, kindness, joy, and peace. You don't have to stay lost in the clouds. In fact, it's time to step out of the storms and enter into the sunbeams of truth, to find deep and abiding love for yourself, and to find your way back to *you*. Imagine the fun this is going to be—especially when you discover that it turns out to be a wondrous version of you that you never knew existed. How exciting! Safe travels, love.

Leaha

About the Author

Leaha Mattinson is a change management specialist, life coach, speaker, and author who "walks her talk" in a truly extraordinary way. In 2008 she learned she would someday inherit Huntington's disease, a genetic, neurological, terminal illness that affects the brain and progressively shuts down the mind and body. It was a devastating diagnosis—yet Leaha realized that to be true to the message she shares with clients, she must live her life consciously with enthusiasm, grace, and gratitude.

She developed her own wellness protocol to halt the onset of the disease by focusing on nutrition, exercise, restorative sleep, mindfulness, and a pervasive sense of reverence for life. But the most crucial attribute of Leaha's success is her mindset: She embraces passion, happiness, and possibility, and turns all negativity into positive life experiences. She attributes her work ethic and values to the example set by her beloved parents and a childhood growing up on a farm where she was immersed in the rhythms of nature.

Her mission is to share these valuable insights with others. As a life and executive coach, she guides her clients toward self-improvement by helping them resolve underlying fears, interrupt bad habits, and break through barriers in order to achieve their goals. She is also a speaker, addressing topics such as stress management, finding courage, discovering purpose, living in uncertainty, and facing terminal illness.

Leaha shares her own life story in her book, *Silver Linings: The Essential Guide to Building Courage, Self-Respect and Wellness.* She is also a radio personality, hosting the show *Master Your Life* on Internet radio, which reaches a global audience. It is aimed at people who are passionate about wellness, personal growth, and self-improvement—those who are eager to bring real change to the way they live and find meaning in a world that's often brutally stressful and disconnected.

Leaha lives on a ranch west of Red Deer, Alberta, with her partner, Dwayne, their blended family, a pack of happy dogs, and a herd of horses.

To learn more about Leaha, visit her website at www.reallifetraining.com.